THE STORY OF
SOJOURNER TRUTH

A Biography Book for New Readers

— Written by —
Anita Crawford Clark

— Illustrated by —
Sawyer Cloud & Simone Douglas

callisto
publishing
an imprint of Sourcebooks

To my aunt, Dr. Margaret Washington,
who first kindled my interest in
Sojourner Truth. To my husband, Darrel,
and our daughters, Janie Rose, Tashia,
and India, and our son-in-law, David,
for your love, prayers, and light. And to
everyone who is a champion for freedom.

Copyright © 2024 by Callisto Publishing LLC
Cover and internal design © 2024 by Callisto Publishing LLC
Illustrations by Sawyer Cloud and Simone Douglas
Photographs by Library of Congress: 50, 53; National Portrait Gallery: 51
Author photo courtesy of Jamie Sutera Photography
Series Designer: Angela Navarra
Art Director: Lisa Realmuto
Art Producer: Maya Melenchuk
Editor: Eliza Kirby
Production Editor: Ruth Sakata Corley
Production Manager: Holly Haydash

Published by Callisto Publishing LLC C/O Sourcebooks LLC
P.O. Box 4410, Naperville, Illinois 60567-4410
(630) 961-3900
callistopublishing.com

Printed and bound in Canada.
Friesens 10 9 8 7 6 5 4 3 2 1

CONTENTS

CHAPTER 1
A Leader Is Born ➜ **1**

8 ⬅ **CHAPTER 2**
The Early Years

CHAPTER 3
Breaking Free ➜ **15**

22 ⬅ **CHAPTER 4**
On a Mission

CHAPTER 5
A New Chapter ➜ **29**

36 ⬅ **CHAPTER 6**
A Strong Supporter

CHAPTER 7
A Voice for Others ➜ **43**

50 ⬅ **CHAPTER 8**
So . . . Who Was Sojourner Truth?

GLOSSARY ➜ **56**

58 ⬅ **BIBLIOGRAPHY**

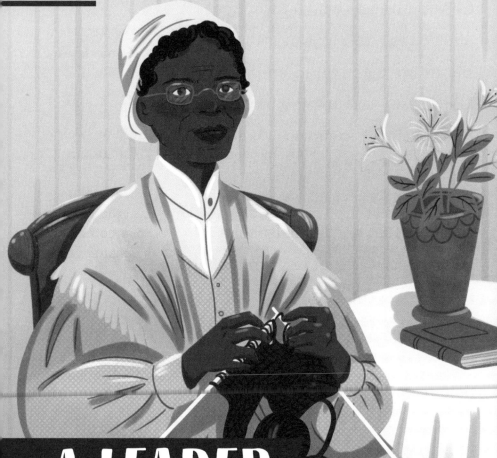

CHAPTER 1

A LEADER IS BORN

☆ **Meet Sojourner Truth** ☆

JUMP IN THE THINK TANK

Sometimes things don't go as planned. Think about a time when things didn't go as planned for you. How did you overcome that challenge?

Can you imagine if you were not allowed to read? When Isabella Baumfree was a child, she was not allowed to learn to read or write. She was born **enslaved**. That meant she was forced to work without pay. She had to do whatever her **enslaver** told her to do. Isabella, however, did not let anything keep her down. When she grew up, she changed her name and became one of the most legendary Americans of all time: Sojourner Truth. Even when she was enslaved, no one could enslave her mind. She was a tower of strength, with a powerful speaking and singing voice. She used these qualities when she decided to set off on a new path of **evangelism**: spreading God's truth.

Although her life took many difficult twists and turns, Sojourner never lost her kindness and courage. She used her voice to not only gain her own freedom, but also to gain freedom and opportunities for others. As an **abolitionist** and activist, Sojourner spoke out against injustices everywhere. Most people will never have an opportunity to meet a United States president, but

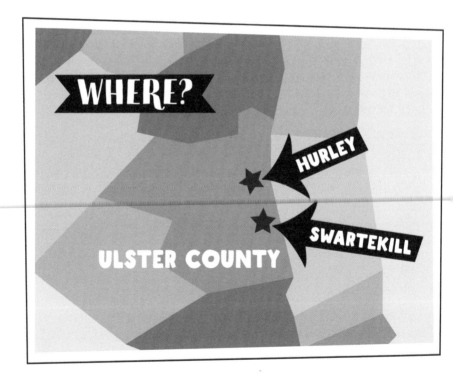

Sojourner Truth met three: Abraham Lincoln, Andrew Johnson, and Ulysses S. Grant. Above all, Sojourner Truth was a **humanitarian**. Even today, we remember her work and her words.

☆ Sojourner's America ☆

Sojourner Truth was born Isabella Baumfree sometime around 1797, in the little town of Hurley in Ulster County, New York. Back then, people did not always keep records for enslaved people, so we do not know her exact date of birth. When Isabella was born, her mother nicknamed her Belle. Her mother and father were James and Elizabeth Baumfree. Belle's mother and father were enslaved, so she was enslaved, too.

Hurley was surrounded by gorgeous meadows and rolling hills. In the distance you could see the towering Catskill and Shawangunk mountains. Little streams helped the nearby forest grow.

This area, so rich in natural beauty, should have been a happy place to grow up. Unfortunately, enslaved people like Isabella and her family had very difficult lives.

> I am **pleading** for my people—
> A poor, down-trodden race,
> Who dwell in **freedom's** boasted
> **land**, with no abiding place.

Enslaved people came from diverse cultures and traditions. Belle's African grandparents made the **Middle Passage** like millions of other Africans. Enslavers took them from their motherland, Africa, and brought them across the ocean in awful conditions on ships. After being separated from their families, Africans were enslaved in the Americas, the Caribbean, and many British colonies. Belle never met her grandparents, but her parents kept their

traditions alive through **oral storytelling**. Passing down stories helped enslaved people stay connected to the motherland. It also gave them strength for the terrible days of enslavement.

WHEN?

George Washington is elected the first U.S. president.

Isabella Baumfree (Sojourner Truth) is born.

1789 —— **1797** ——

Abraham Lincoln is born.

Abolitionist Frederick Douglass is born.

1809 —— **1817** ——

CHAPTER 2

THE EARLY YEARS

Belle was too young to remember her first enslaver. His name was Colonel Johannes Hardenbergh Jr. The Hardenbergh **estate** was in Swartekill, New York. Everyone on the Hardenbergh estate spoke **Dutch**, so it

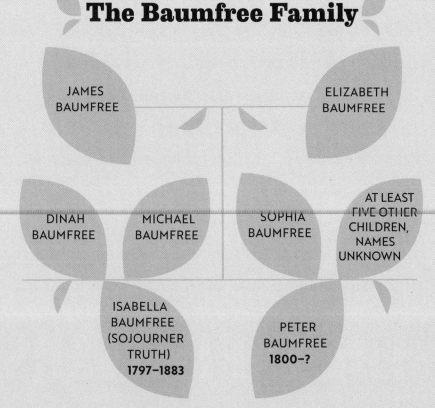

The Baumfree Family

JAMES BAUMFREE

ELIZABETH BAUMFREE

DINAH BAUMFREE

MICHAEL BAUMFREE

SOPHIA BAUMFREE

AT LEAST FIVE OTHER CHILDREN, NAMES UNKNOWN

ISABELLA BAUMFREE (SOJOURNER TRUTH) **1797–1883**

PETER BAUMFREE **1800–?**

was Isabella's first language. She did not learn English until she was older. After Johannes Hardenbergh died, his son Charles inherited all his property. This inheritance included his father's land and house, as well as all the people he enslaved. Belle, her family, and the other enslaved people were taken to live in Charles's home. The only place for them to sleep was in the cellar on damp floorboards.

Belle was around five years old when she started working alongside her mother. She learned how to wash, sew, knit, cook, and garden.

Her enslavers hoped these housekeeping skills would make her more valuable when she grew up.

Belle's mother, known as Mau-Mau Bet, often spoke to God through prayer. She taught Belle and her little brother Peter to ask God for help when they were mistreated. Belle's father, James, was nicknamed Baumfree. *Baum* means "tree" in Dutch. He was tall like a tree. Baumfree and Mau-Mau Bet had as many as 10 other children. They were sold away one by one. Enslavers did not always keep families together. They sold enslaved people to make money or to settle debts. Belle and Peter were fortunate to live with their parents longer than their brothers and sisters.

☆ Saying Goodbye ☆

In 1808, Charles Hardenbergh died. Belle was about 11 years old. Mau-Mau Bet feared that Belle and Peter would soon be sold away from her. Sadly, that day arrived in early 1810. Belle was sold with a flock

of sheep for $100 to a man named John Neely Jr. Peter was sold, too. Baumfree and Mau-Mau Bet were too old to be sold. They were freed and allowed to keep living in the Hardenbergh cellar.

The Neelys were an unkind family. They spoke only English. Belle spoke only Dutch. When Belle did not understand their commands, they beat her. The Neelys did not give Belle any warm clothing or shoes. She had to go barefoot, even in the winter. She got terrible **frostbite**. One Sunday, Neely beat Belle so badly, it scarred her for life. Belle was sad and all alone. Thankfully, she remembered her mother's teachings. Mau-Mau Bet had taught Belle to ask God to "protect and shield her from her **persecutors**."

JUMP
IN THE
THINK
TANK

Learning a new language can be challenging. Have you ever learned a skill that you once thought you'd never learn?

One day, an answer to Belle's prayers appeared. Her father walked 15 miles to visit her. When Baumfree saw Belle's injuries and her frostbitten feet, he was horrified. He promised he would find her a better place to live. Each day, Belle walked in the footprints her father had left in the snow. Baumfree kept his word. Soon Martinus Schryver bought Belle.

The Schryvers were still enslavers, but they were kinder than the Neelys. They spoke both Dutch and English. Belle learned to speak English, too. A few months later, the Schryvers fell on hard times and had to sell Belle.

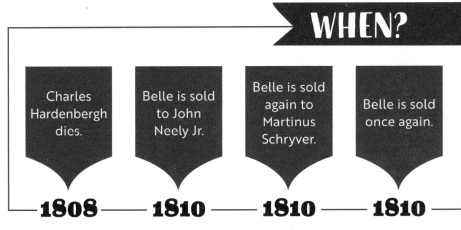

CHAPTER 3

BREAKING FREE

☆ The Dumont Farm ☆

In 1810, when she was about 13 years old, Belle was sold again. John Dumont of New Paltz, New York, bought her. Belle's day began at dawn. She lit a fire to warm the house, gathered water, prepared breakfast, milked the cows, and collected eggs. Soon Belle also worked in the fields. She was nearly six feet tall. Dumont often bragged about Belle's strength and hard work.

Everyone in the Dumont home spoke Dutch. Still Belle was not comfortable there. Mrs. Dumont disliked her. She encouraged her white maids to make Belle's life difficult. Once a white servant named Kate ruined the breakfast potatoes and blamed Belle. The Dumonts scolded Belle harshly. But Dumont's 10-year-old daughter, Gertrude, had seen Kate throwing ashes in the kettle of boiling potatoes.

JUMP
—IN THE—
THINK
TANK

Belle often felt alone, but one small act of kindness touched her heart. Has anyone ever shown you a small act of kindness?

She told her father and cleared Belle's name. Gertrude's kind act touched Belle's heart.

When Belle was older, she fell in love with an enslaved man named Robert from a neighboring farm. Robert's enslaver, Charles Catton Jr., forbid them to have a relationship. He knew if Belle had any children, they would belong to Dumont. Robert

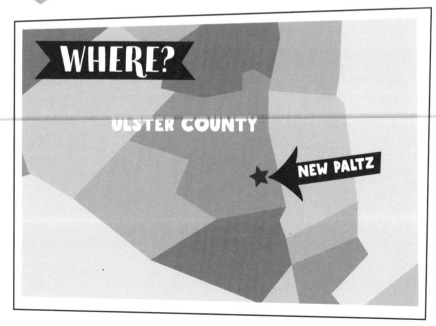

WHERE?

ULSTER COUNTY

NEW PALTZ

and Belle never saw each other again. Belle
eventually married Thomas, an enslaved man
on Dumont's farm. Thomas and Belle had
three children named Peter, Elizabeth, and
Sophia. Before their marriage, Belle had two
other children. Her firstborn, James, died in
childhood. Historians do not know for sure who
his father was. They believe John Dumont was
the father of Belle's second baby, Diana.

☆ **A Broken Promise** ☆

As Belle settled into life with the Dumonts, her world was changing. Both her parents had died. She now had a husband and children. And she could not believe what would happen next: New York was planning to **abolish**, or end, slavery. The law stated that enslaved people born before July 4, 1799, would be freed on July 4, 1827. That group included Belle and Thomas but not their children, who were born after 1799 and would have to wait. John Dumont promised Belle he would grant her freedom in 1826, one year early. He also promised to build Belle and Thomas a little cabin for their family. When John Dumont broke his promise, Belle was very angry. She decided to leave the Dumont farm and claim her own freedom.

It was not an easy decision. Belle would have to leave her older children behind with Thomas. Belle prayed to God for guidance. Early one autumn morning in 1826, Belle left the Dumont farm with only a knapsack and her baby Sophia. She made her way to the home of Isaac Van Wagenen. The Van Wagenens were abolitionists. They thought slavery was wrong and wanted it outlawed. Belle had known the Van Wagenens

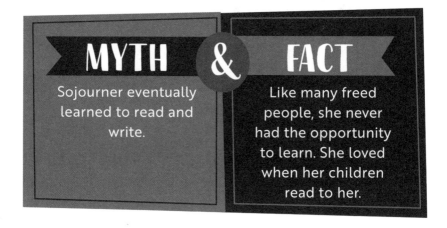

MYTH & FACT

MYTH: Sojourner eventually learned to read and write.

FACT: Like many freed people, she never had the opportunity to learn. She loved when her children read to her.

as a child. They helped her buy her freedom from John Dumont. To mark her new status as a free woman, she changed her name to Isabella Van Wagenen.

WHEN?

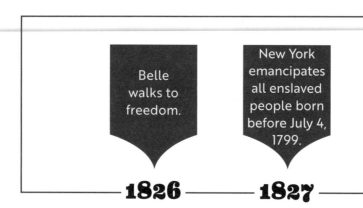

Belle walks to freedom.

New York emancipates all enslaved people born before July 4, 1799.

1826 — **1827**

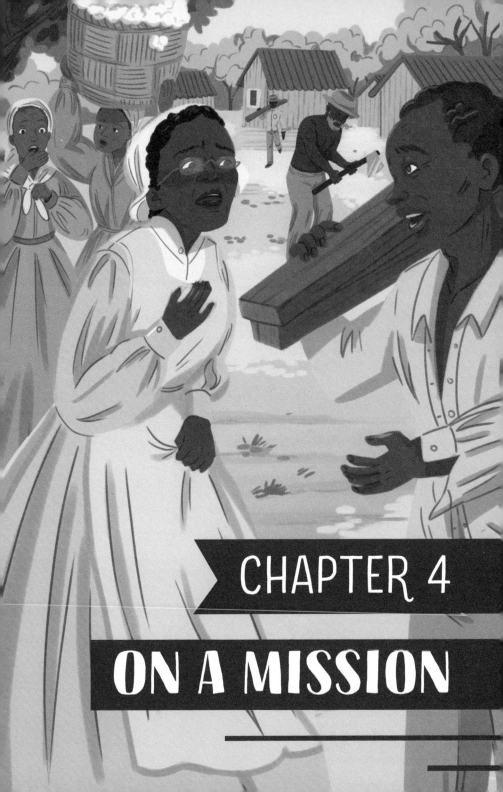

CHAPTER 4

ON A MISSION

☆ Saving Peter ☆

Belle was happy to be free, but she soon got terrible news. John Dumont had sold her five-year-old son, Peter. New York's **emancipation** law stated that all enslaved children had to remain in the state until they were old enough to be freed. Peter would not be free until he turned 28. Peter's new enslaver, Solomon Gidney, broke the law and took him to Alabama. When enslaved people were taken to the South, they were often never seen or heard from again.

Belle wasted no time trying to get Peter back. She walked the dusty country roads, letting everyone know what happened to her son. Nobody would help her. Finally, some kind **Quakers** helped her file a **lawsuit** to have her son returned. While she waited for a court date, Belle spoke out on the cruelties of slavery. She soon met a lawyer in Kingston, New York, named Herman M. Romeyn. He arranged a special court hearing that forced Gidney to show up with Peter in New York.

Peter had been whipped, kicked, and beaten by his Alabama enslavers. He was terrified they would hurt him more. He was so afraid he would not even say that Belle was his mother. Still, the judge returned Peter to Belle and declared him free.

Belle had her son once again, but Peter would never be the same. Belle became one of the first Black women to bring a court case against a white man—and win!

> Oh my God! I know'd I'd have **him** again. I was sure God would help me to get him. **Why**, I felt so **tall** within—I felt as if the power of a **nation** was with me!

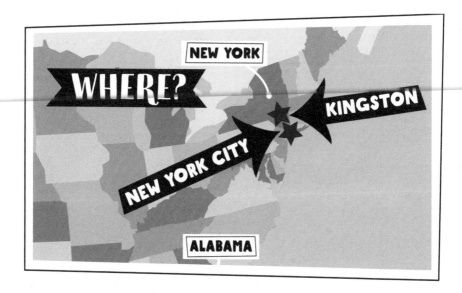

☆ **Teaching and Preaching** ☆

With her son back, Belle stayed in Kingston
with the Van Wagenens. Thomas stayed with
their daughters Diana and Elizabeth at the
Dumonts. In 1827, Thomas was freed. But he was
in poor health, and he soon died.

In April 1827, Belle had a life-changing
religious experience. Mau-Mau Bet had taught
her spiritual traditions from Africa when she
was child. She had also learned about different

JUMP
IN THE
THINK TANK

Belle was overjoyed to be reunited with her siblings. Have you ever found something you thought was lost? How did you feel?

Christian teachings. Yet Belle felt something was missing. One night she had a vision of God. Afterward, she said she truly understood His power and might. Belle began **preaching**, sharing God's word.

In 1828, Belle moved to New York City with Peter. She worked for a Christian family as a housekeeper. Before long, she began meeting Black community leaders. By 1831, she joined the African Methodist Episcopal Zion Church. There she was joyfully reunited with two of her siblings, Sophia and Michael. Sadly, another sister, Dinah, had recently died. Belle realized she and Dinah had prayed together at Zion, but Belle had not known Dinah was her sister. Belle, Sophia, and Michael all cried together.

Belle asked, "Oh Lord, what is this slavery . . .
What evil can it not do?"

Belle began teaching and preaching in New
York's poorest neighborhoods. She boldly went
where other women activists feared to visit. She
began to learn about other causes, like women's
rights and **temperance**, which meant banning
alcohol. She also held private prayer meetings,
organized and taught Sabbath schools, and
handed out Bibles. Belle continued this work for
11 years.

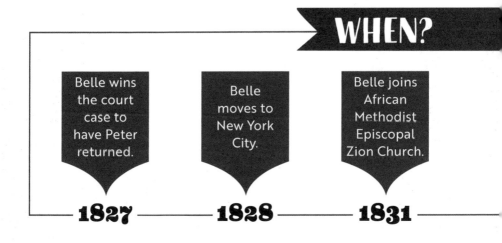

WHEN?

Belle wins the court case to have Peter returned.

Belle moves to New York City.

Belle joins African Methodist Episcopal Zion Church.

1827 — 1828 — 1831 —

CHAPTER 5

A NEW CHAPTER

From Isabella to
☆ Sojourner Truth ☆

One sleepless night, Belle was troubled and prayed deeply. She heard a voice say, *Leave the city—go east.* God was calling her to travel and preach the truth. On June 1, 1843, at 46 years old, Belle left New York City for Long Island. She changed her name to Sojourner, which means "traveler." She left with just a few clothes and very little money.

On Long Island, Sojourner walked along the dusty road and soon grew thirsty. She met a Quaker woman and asked for a drink of water. The Quaker woman asked her name. She answered, "Sojourner." Then the woman wanted to know, "Sojourner what?"

Sojourner hadn't thought about a new last name. She cried out, "Oh God, give me a name with a handle to it." Then it came to her.

She was devoting herself to spreading the truth. Her name would be Sojourner Truth.

Sojourner preached throughout the Northeast. She told her story and spoke out against slavery. Sojourner was a powerful presence. When a mob disrupted a camp meeting in Northampton, the organizers feared for everyone's safety. But Sojourner began singing in her strongest voice. The mob settled down and listened as she sang and preached. The mob soon left in peace.

Sojourner Truth met abolitionist leaders like Frederick Douglass and William Lloyd Garrison. Sojourner didn't shy away from challenging these great leaders in public when she disagreed with them. They respected her words and beliefs.

In 1850, Sojourner Truth **dictated** her autobiography to her friend Olive Gilbert. It was called the *Narrative of Sojourner Truth: A Northern Slave.*

JUMP
—IN THE—
THINK TANK

Speaking in front of people is not always easy. Think of a time when you had to do something difficult. How did you get through it?

> There is a **holy** city,
> A world of light above,
> **Above** the starry regions
> Built by the God of **love**.
>
> **—SOJOURNER'S FAVORITE HYMN**

☆ Sojourner Speaks ☆

In 1851, Garrison invited Sojourner on a speaking tour through New York with abolitionist George Thompson. Garrison told her she would be able to sell her books. Sojourner's meetings drew large groups of both Black and white listeners. Her stories of enslavement made people sit up and pay attention.

Later that year, at the Ohio Women's Rights Convention in Akron, Ohio, Sojourner gave a famous speech. The speech was called

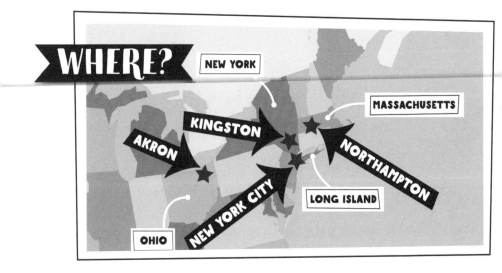

WHERE?

NEW YORK

MASSACHUSETTS

KINGSTON

AKRON

NORTHAMPTON

NEW YORK CITY

LONG ISLAND

OHIO

"Ain't I a Woman?" Sojourner spoke about the rights of all women. She said women should be treated equal to men. Several versions of this speech have been printed. Some publishers made Sojourner sound like she spoke with a southern accent. But remember, she was from New York. She would have had a Dutch accent.

During her travels, Sojourner faced hardships. Pro-slavery groups, who did not want slavery to end, **protested** her speeches. Even in the

face of angry mobs, she did not quit. She drew strength from her faith. Around the time her book came out, a law called the Fugitive Slave Act of 1850 passed. It stated that citizens could help capture runaway slaves. But people called "men-stealers" were kidnapping free Black people and forcing them into enslavement. Many Black people fled to Canada. Sojourner kept a keen eye out for potential men-stealers. She knew she had to work even harder now to protect her people.

WHEN?

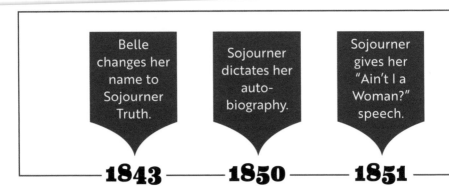

Belle changes her name to Sojourner Truth.

Sojourner dictates her auto-biography.

Sojourner gives her "Ain't I a Woman?" speech.

1843 —— 1850 —— 1851 ——

CHAPTER 6

A STRONG SUPPORTER

☆ The Civil War ☆

In July 1857, Sojourner Truth moved to a farming village called Harmonia, near Battle Creek, Michigan. Black and white people lived side by side as neighbors. Some of Sojourner's family lived with her. She especially enjoyed time with her two grandsons, Sammy and James. Harmonia was also an important stop on the **Underground Railroad**, which helped Southern enslaved people escape.

In 1860, Abraham Lincoln was elected president of the United States. He was against the spread of slavery. After his election, 11 Southern states **seceded** from the rest of the United States. They formed the **Confederate States of America**. The South wanted slavery to continue. The North, or **Union**, wanted to end slavery in the entire country. Both sides believed strongly in their causes. Then the Confederates fired the first shots on Fort Sumter. This began the **American Civil War** in 1861. Sojourner did not believe in violence. Still, she supported the Union on their road to victory.

During the Civil War, Sojourner signed up soldiers for the Union army. She organized and gathered supplies for Black troops and volunteers. Unfortunately, Black troops were not treated equally, even in the Union Army. They still fought with courage and honor. Lincoln knew about Sojourner's hard work. On October 29, 1864, Sojourner met with him.

Some of the Black soldiers she had helped were set free by the **Emancipation Proclamation** he signed on January 1, 1863. It freed all enslaved people in the Confederate States. She told Lincoln that he was "the best president who has ever taken the seat."

Giving Back and ☆ Speaking Out ☆

In 1864, Sojourner worked with the National Freedman's Relief Association in Washington, D.C. She worked at the Freedman's Village, a community for freed Black people. Sojourner was horrified by their living conditions. They lived in shacks, had only rags for clothing, and often went hungry. Sojourner helped them build new lives.

The Civil War ended on April 9, 1865. The Union won, but it would take time for the nation to heal. Sojourner's grandson James had fought for the Union. He was released from a Confederate prison at the end of the war. Just like her son Peter, he had suffered greatly. Sojourner was heartbroken to see his pain.

Sojourner continued her work with the freed people. The war was over, but **segregation** became a problem. People were separated by their skin color. This separation was never equal.

JUMP IN THE THINK TANK

Sojourner loved helping people and seeing them treated fairly. Why do you think that was?

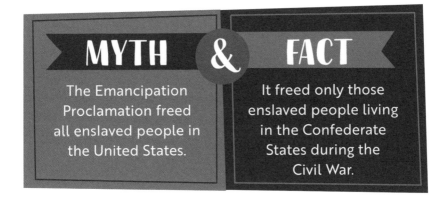

MYTH & FACT

The Emancipation Proclamation freed all enslaved people in the United States.

It freed only those enslaved people living in the Confederate States during the Civil War.

Sojourner was now in her late sixties. She worked as hard as ever at the Freedmen's Hospital. She nursed the sick. She looked after homeless elderly people and visited orphanages. The freed people called Sojourner an "angel of mercy" because of her devotion.

To get around, Sojourner sometimes took streetcars. This made the conductors very angry. They did not want Black passengers to ride on streetcars with white passengers. Conductors tried to throw Sojourner off several times. She reported what happened. One case went to trial. Sojourner's actions led to the **integration** of the transportation system in Washington, D.C. It meant other conductors had to allow Black passengers to ride.

WHERE?

MICHIGAN

BATTLE CREEK

WASHINGTON, D.C.

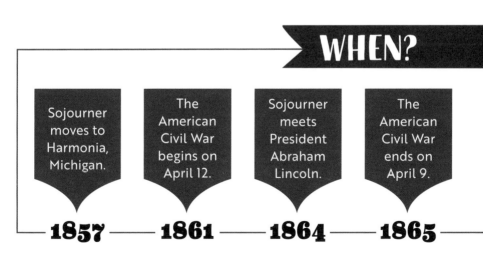

WHEN?

Sojourner moves to Harmonia, Michigan.	The American Civil War begins on April 12.	Sojourner meets President Abraham Lincoln.	The American Civil War ends on April 9.
1857	**1861**	**1864**	**1865**

CHAPTER 7

A VOICE FOR OTHERS

☆ Justice for All ☆

Friends wanted Sojourner to slow down and
rest. But Sojourner believed God kept her in
good health so she could continue her work. The
horrible living conditions at the Freedman's
Village disturbed Sojourner. She urged freed
people to move. She and other supporters helped
hundreds of freed people move to better places.

Sojourner began to fight for the government
to give land to formerly enslaved men and
women. She felt Black people could never be
truly free unless they could do well financially,
too. Even when other leaders gave up on the idea
of land for freed people, Sojourner kept going.
For seven years, she pled for support for freed
people. She took her cause to Washington, D.C.
Sojourner could not understand why Congress
was unwilling to take action. After all, enslaved
Black labor had made white America **wealthy**.

Sojourner had the opportunity to meet with President Ulysses S. Grant in the White House. She became active in Grant's re-election **campaign**. Later Sojourner celebrated and spoke in Washington, D.C. when Grant passed the Fifteenth Amendment, which allowed Black men to vote. Women, however, were still not allowed to vote. Sojourner continued to speak on many topics. She spoke about women's rights. She spoke on prison reform and integration. She spoke about temperance. She spoke well into the later years of her life. Sojourner Truth was one of America's most passionate champions for human rights. She gave her last major speech in June 1881, in Michigan.

☆ Sojourner's Legacy ☆

Sojourner's health began to decline, but her mind was still sharp. Her daughters Diana and Elizabeth took care of her. She enjoyed visits with friends, family, and news reporters. On November 26, 1883, Sojourner Truth passed away. Flowers, poems, and tributes were sent in her honor. More than 1,000 people attended Sojourner's funeral. She was buried in Oak Hill Cemetery. The *Battle Creek Journal* wrote, "The work which she achieved will be treasured in the hearts of the great body of our people and will have a lasting place on the pages of history."

Sojourner Truth will be remembered as one of the most important leaders of the abolition movement. She was a champion for civil rights and social justice. She was also outspoken about temperance and women's rights. Sadly, she did not live to see women gain the right to vote. The Nineteenth Amendment, which gave women the right to vote, was not approved until 1920. It was nearly 40 years after Sojourner Truth's death.

Sojourner Truth's **legacy** is still very much alive today. Women continue to work for equality in many areas. Black people still fight racism and unfair voting laws. Human rights, prison reform, and health care reform are still important causes. More than anything, Sojourner Truth was a humanitarian. Many monuments, statues, and works of art have been created to honor this remarkable woman.

JUMP IN THE THINK TANK

Sojourner had many accomplishments. What do you think was her greatest accomplishment? Why?

WHEN?

Sojourner gives her last major speech.

Sojourner dies on November 26.

1881 —— **1883** —

CHAPTER 8

SO . . . WHO WAS SOJOURNER TRUTH?

☆ **Challenge Accepted!** ☆

Now that you know so much about Sojourner Truth's dynamic life and legacy, let's see what you've learned with this fun little quiz. There are 10 questions to test your new knowledge. Feel free to look back in the book to find the answers if you need to, but try to remember first!

1 | **Where was Sojourner born?**
→ A   Battle Creek, Michigan
→ B   Washington, D.C.
→ C   Ulster County, New York
→ D   Harmonia, Michigan

2 | **What was Sojourner's first name before she changed it?**
→ A   Elizabeth
→ B   Isabella
→ C   Sophia
→ D   Getty

3 **What was Sojourner's first language?**

→ A English

→ B Dutch

→ C Spanish

→ D French

4 **About how tall was Sojourner Truth as a grown woman?**

→ A 5 feet, 5 inches

→ B 6 feet, 5 inches

→ C 6 feet

→ D 5 feet

5 **When Sojourner walked to freedom with her baby Sophia, whose home did she end up going to?**

→ A Isaac Van Wagenen

→ B John Dumont

→ C Martinus Schryver

→ D John Neely Jr.

6 **Why did Sojourner change her name from Isabella Van Wagenen to Sojourner Truth?**

→ A   She thought it sounded more professional.

→ B   One of her fellow abolitionists suggested it to her.

→ C   She had a new calling from God to travel and preach the truth.

→ D   She did not like the name given her by her enslavers.

7 **When Dumont sold Peter, where did his enslavers take him?**

→ A   Georgia

→ B   Mississippi

→ C   Virginia

→ D   Alabama

8 **What was Sojourner Truth's most notable accomplishment?**

→ A   Dictating her book *The Narrative of Sojourner Truth*

→ B   Winning the court case to have her son Peter returned to her

→ C   Winning cases against conductors for the right to ride on streetcars in Washington, D.C.

→ D   All of the above

9 **Who was the first United States president Sojourner Truth met?**

→ A Ulysses S. Grant

→ B George Washington

→ C Abraham Lincoln

→ D Thomas Jefferson

10 **How did Sojourner Truth change the world?**

→ A She was a leading abolitionist and champion for women's rights.

→ B She was an early leader fighting for the rights of Black people, women, and humanity.

→ C She used money from her speeches, singing, book sales, and photos to help newly freed Black people start new lives.

→ D All of the above

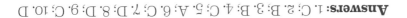

☆ **Our World** ☆

Sojourner Truth is considered one of the most remarkable Black women of the 19th century. It has been nearly 140 years since her death, but we still feel the impact of her work today.

→ Sojourner Truth was an early supporter of women's rights. Women today say, "Women's rights are human rights." It means fair treatment for women is fair treatment for everyone. Few understood this concept better than Sojourner. She fought for women's rights during her lifetime, knowing it would matter for women today.

→ Sojourner Truth took a stand when she boarded a streetcar in Washington, D.C. When she refused to leave, the conductor tried to throw her off. On December 1, 1955, Rosa Parks refused to give up her bus seat to a white man. This act of courage sparked the civil rights movement.

→ Sojourner Truth spoke out against injustice wherever she found it. She spoke up for freedom and human rights. She did not let her background, or speaking English as a second language, or not being able to read and write stop her. Sojourner blazed a trail for all humanity.

JUMP
—IN THE—
THINK TANK
FOR
MORE!

Now let's think a little bit more about Sojourner Truth's life and how she changed the world.

→ Sojourner's life changed when she decided to emancipate herself by walking to freedom. Do you think she would have gone on to do such remarkable things if she had remained enslaved on Dumont's farm?

→ Things did not always turn out the way Sojourner hoped, but she always found ways to keep moving forward. How have you found ways to keep moving forward even when things did not go your way?

→ Sojourner Truth accomplished things that seemed impossible. Have you or someone you know ever accomplished something that seemed impossible?

Glossary

abolish: To put an end to something

abolitionist: A person who wanted slavery to be outlawed

American Civil War: The war in the United States between the Southern states and the Northern states from 1861 to 1865

campaign: Activities and actions that are meant to help a person who is running for political office get elected

Confederate States of America: The 11 states that seceded from the Union during the American Civil War

dictated: Said aloud for another person to write down

Dutch: A language usually spoken by people of the Netherlands and northern Belgium

emancipation: Being freed

Emancipation Proclamation: Law signed by President Abraham Lincoln, declaring "all persons held as slaves" within the rebellious states "are, and henceforward shall be, free"

enslaved: Forced to work without the freedom to choose and without pay

enslaver: Someone who enslaves another person and treats them like property

estate: A large area of land with a big house

evangelism: Spreading Christianity by preaching God's word

frostbite: A condition in which parts of the body, like fingers or toes, are damaged as a result of being very cold

humanitarian: A person who works to help everyone have better lives

integration: The end of a policy that keeps people apart, usually based on their race or skin color

lawsuit: A dispute between people or groups of people that is taken to a court to decide

legacy: Something a person leaves behind for which they are remembered

Middle Passage: The journey in which millions of Africans were forced to ride in inhumane conditions on ships from Africa to the Americas

oral storytelling: Telling a story aloud through poems, chants, rhymes, songs, and more

persecutors: People who treat a particular person or group of people cruelly

preaching: Speaking about the Bible, religion, or faith

protested: An action to show that you disagree with something

Quakers: A group of Christians who believe in peace and dress plainly

seceded: Left or pulled out of a group

segregation: The separation of people, usually based on their race or skin color

temperance: A movement against drinking alcohol

Underground Railroad: A secret network of safe houses that enslaved people used to escape slavery

Union: The Northern states that stayed together after the Southern states seceded

wealthy: Having plenty or being rich

Bibliography

Fitch, Suzanne Pullon, and Roseann M. Mandziuk. *Sojourner Truth as Orator: Wit, Story, and Song.* Westport, CT: Greenwood Press, 1997.

Painter, Nell Irvin. *Sojourner Truth: A Life, a Symbol.* New York: W. W. Norton & Company, 1996.

Truth, Sojourner, et al. *Narrative of Sojourner Truth: A Bondswoman of Olden Time, with a History of Her Labors and Correspondence Drawn from Her Book of Life; Also, a Memorial Chapter.* New York: Penguin Books, 1998.

Washington, Margaret. *Sojourner Truth's America.* Champaign, IL: University of Illinois Press, 2009.

About the Author

Anita Crawford Clark is a writer and illustrator of fiction and nonfiction books for children. Anita grew up chasing butterflies and fishing for crawdads from a nearby creek during scorching Sacramento summers. Her stories and illustrations often reflect those memorable childhood years. Her debut picture book, *Old to Joy*, draws on those fond memories. A veteran K-12 teacher, Anita especially enjoys directing musical theatre productions. The athlete in Anita enjoys shooting hoops. The musician in her enjoys playing the drums, piano, and banjo. Anita draws inspiration from her faith, nature, music, history, and everyday life. You can find out more about Anita and her books at anitacrawfordclark.com.

About the Illustrators

Sawyer Cloud is a self-taught artist living in Madagascar, her birth country. Previous titles include *The Juneteenth Story* by Alliah L. Agostini, *Sugar Pie Lullaby* by Carole Boston Weatherford, among many others.

Simone Douglas is a full-time illustrator and digital artist based in London who specialises in book illustrations, particularly young adult fiction and cover art. She's a gamer at heart, and when she's not catching up with her TV shows, you can find her out in nature.

WHO WILL INSPIRE YOU NEXT?

EXPLORE A WORLD OF HEROES AND ROLE MODELS IN
THE STORY OF... BIOGRAPHY SERIES FOR NEW READERS.

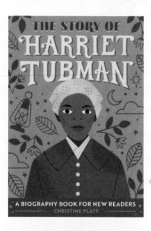

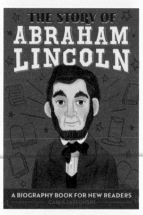

LOOK FOR THIS SERIES
WHEREVER BOOKS AND EBOOKS ARE SOLD

Alexander Hamilton	Jane Goodall
Albert Einstein	Barack Obama
Ruby Bridges	Helen Keller
George Washington	Marie Curie